A CHILD'S HISTORY OF ENGLAND

the notebook edition

Colour the Classics

xoxo

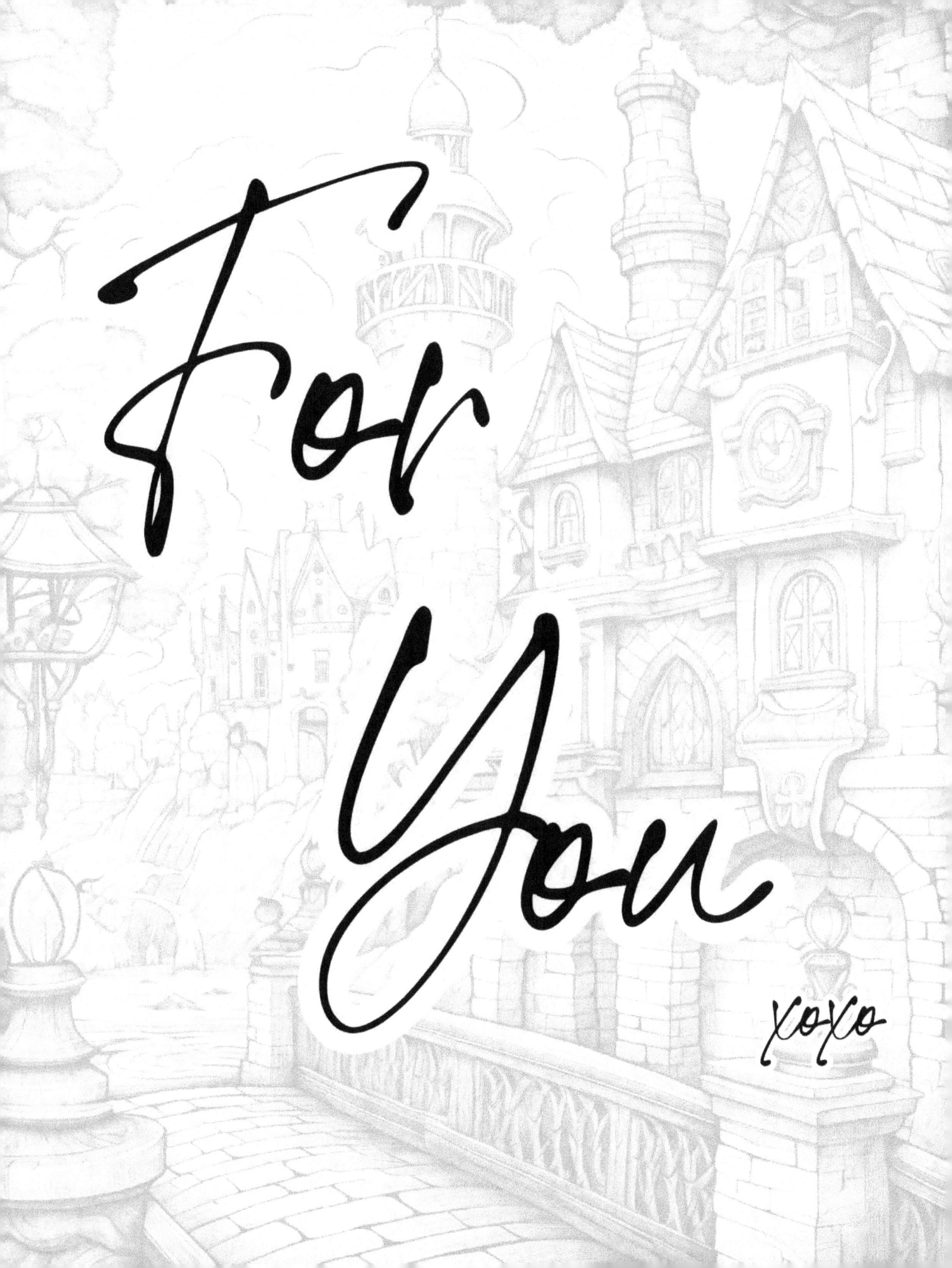
For You
xoxo

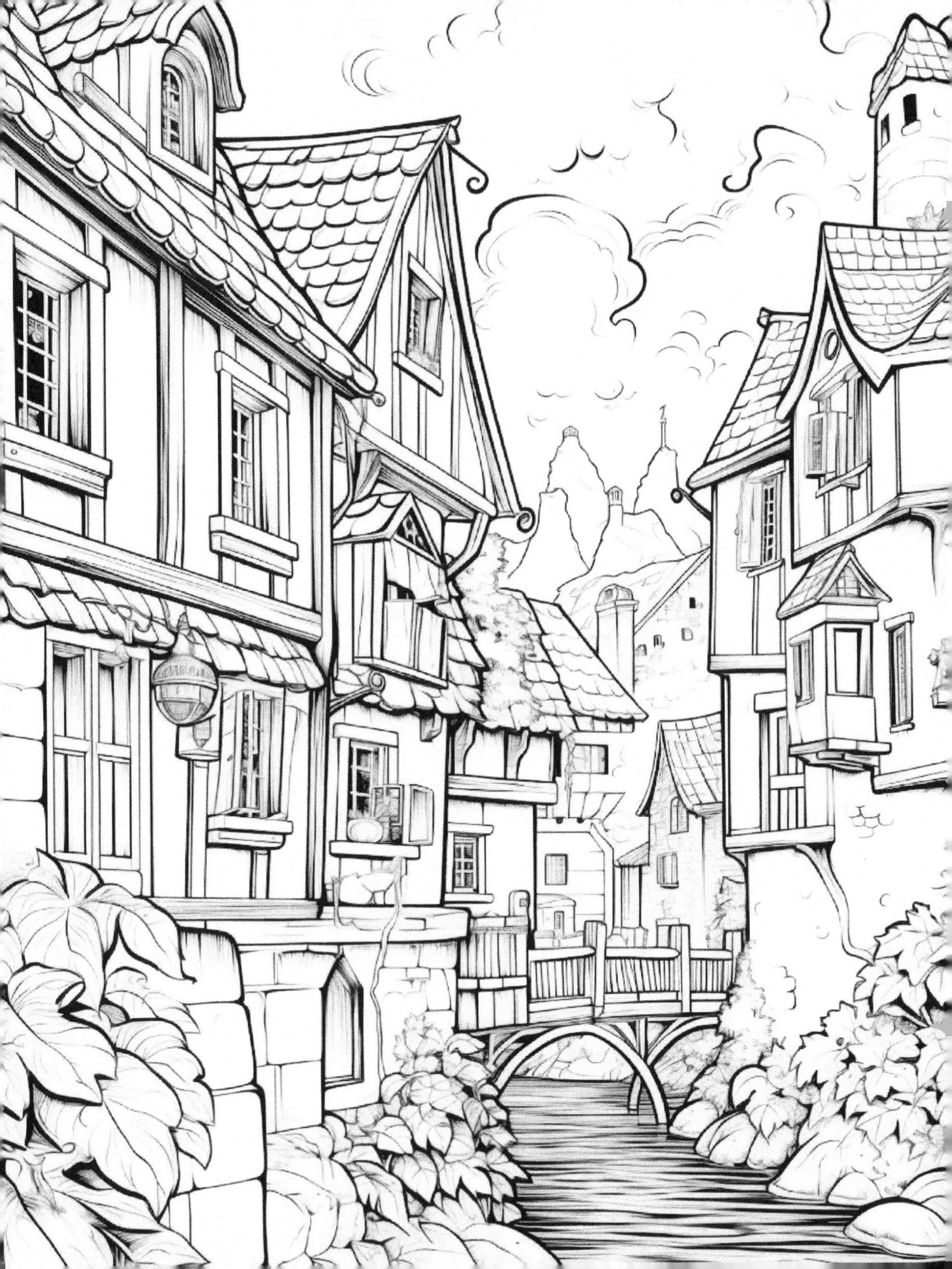

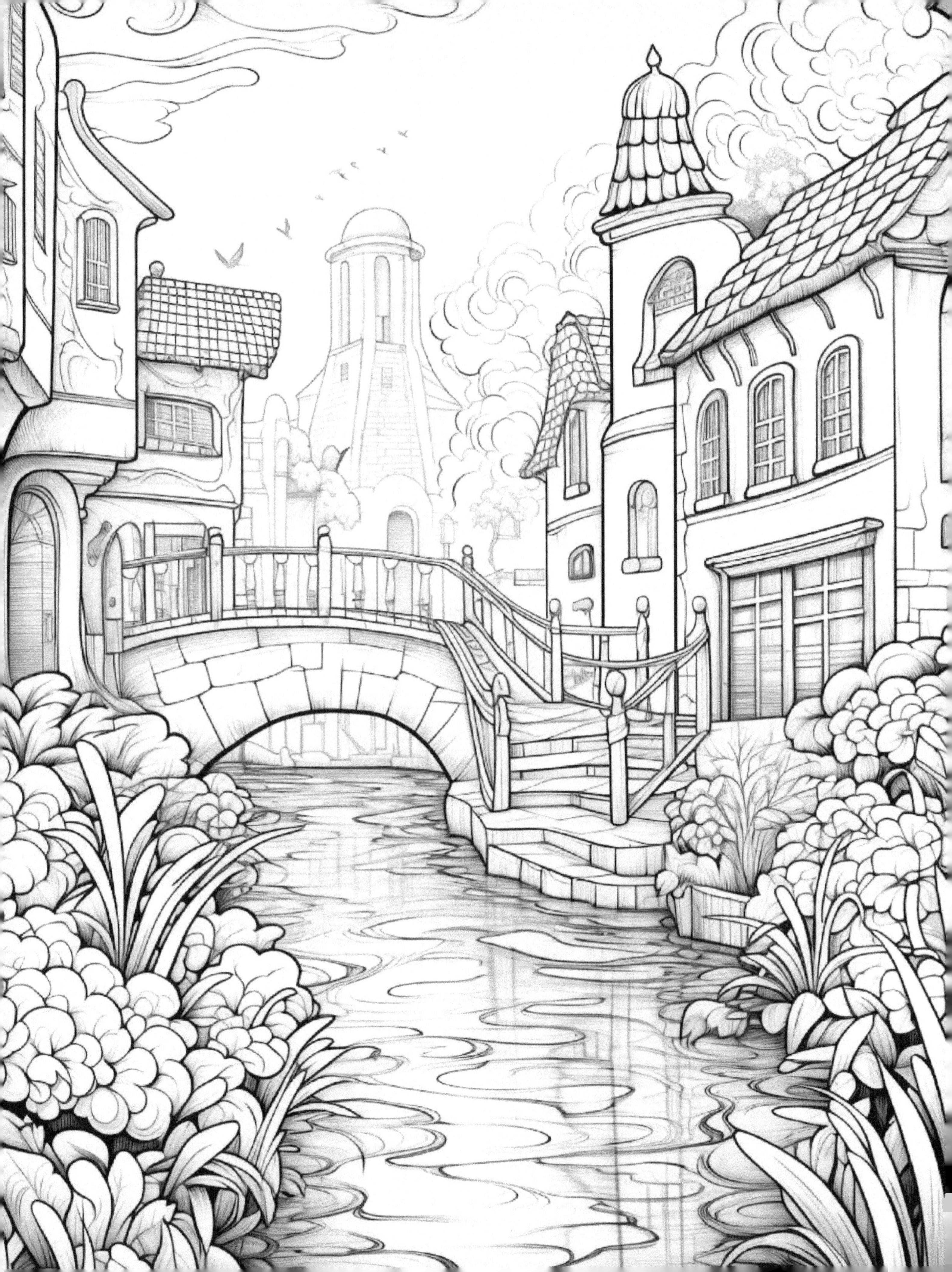

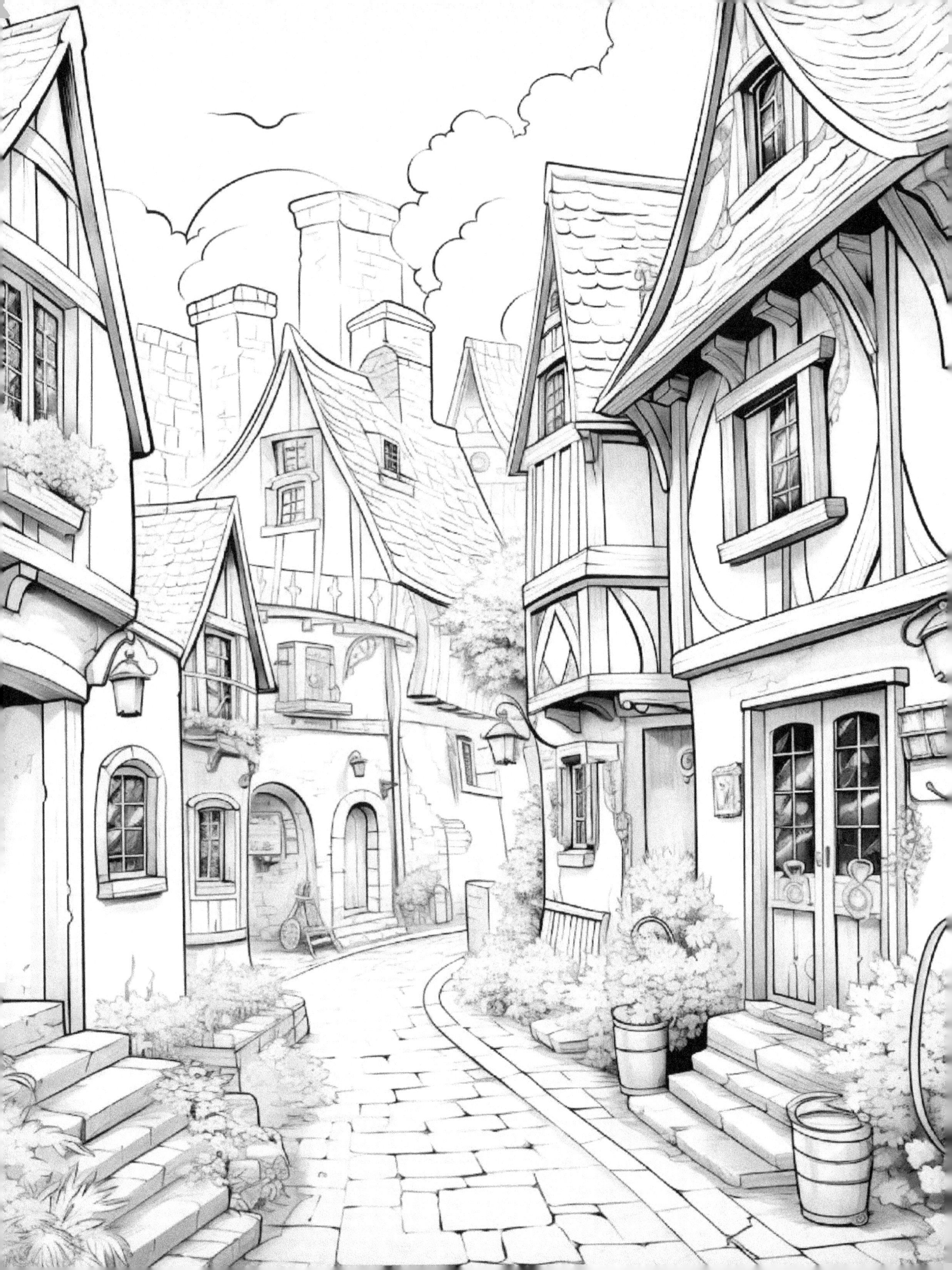

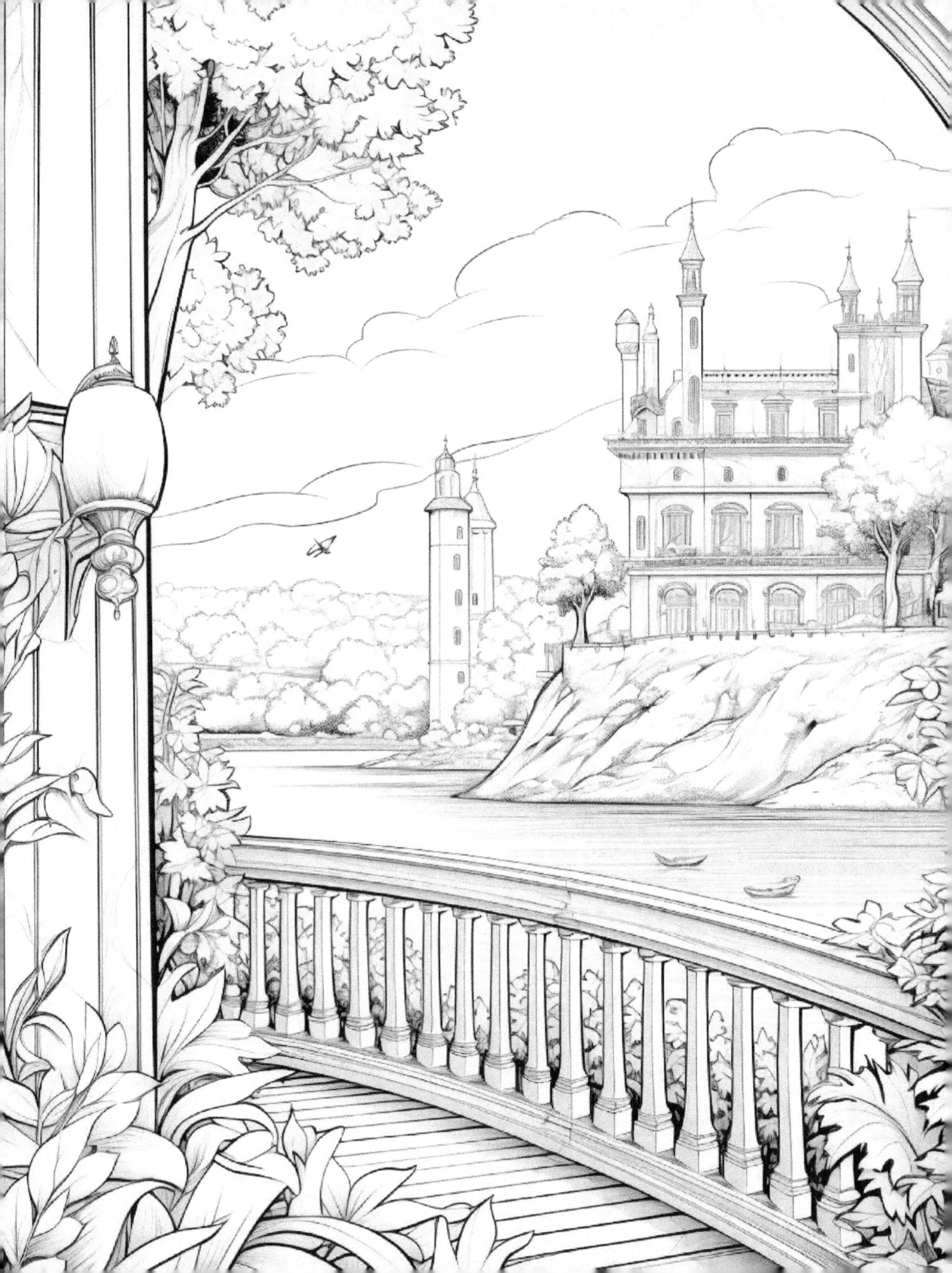

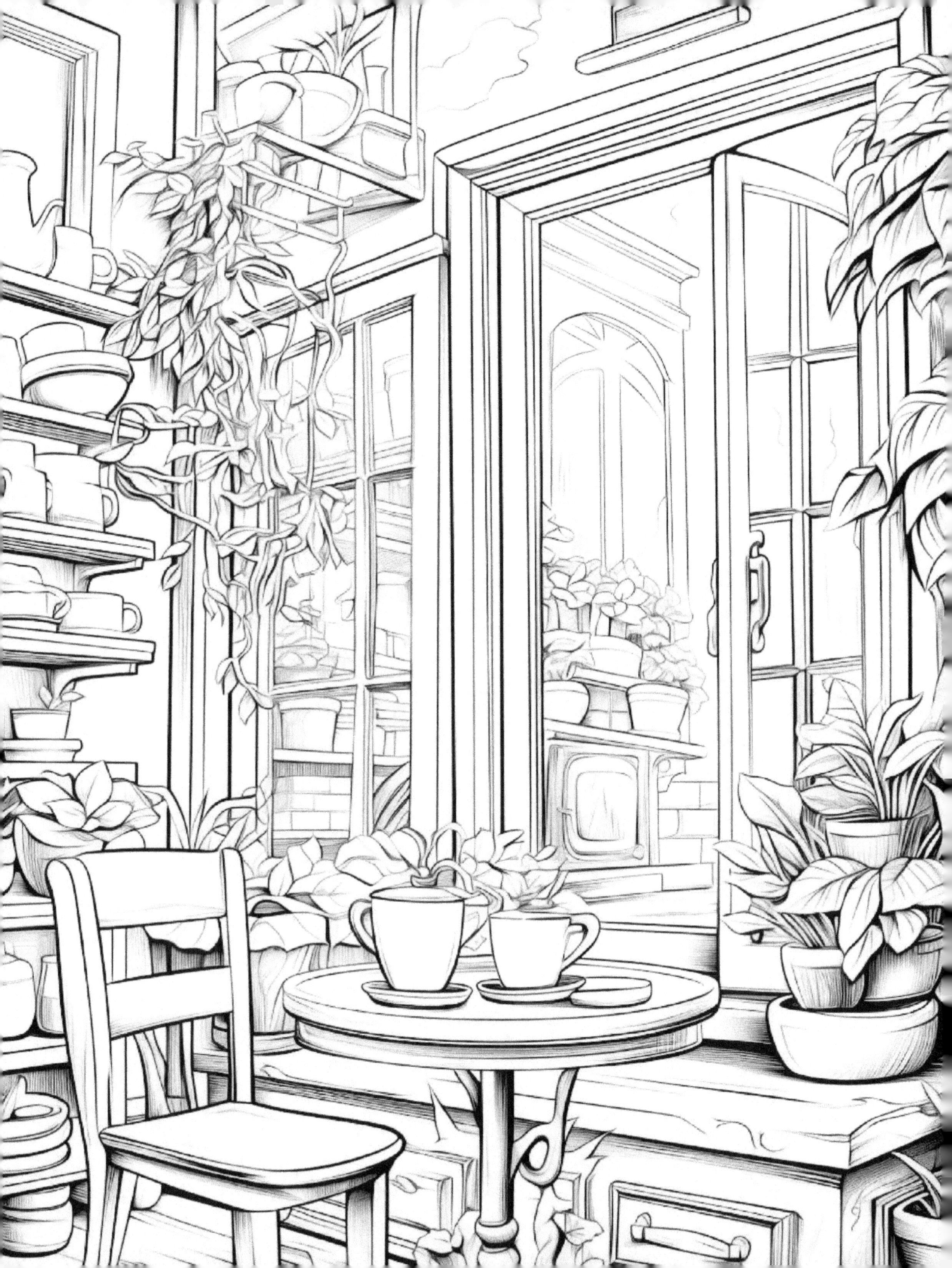

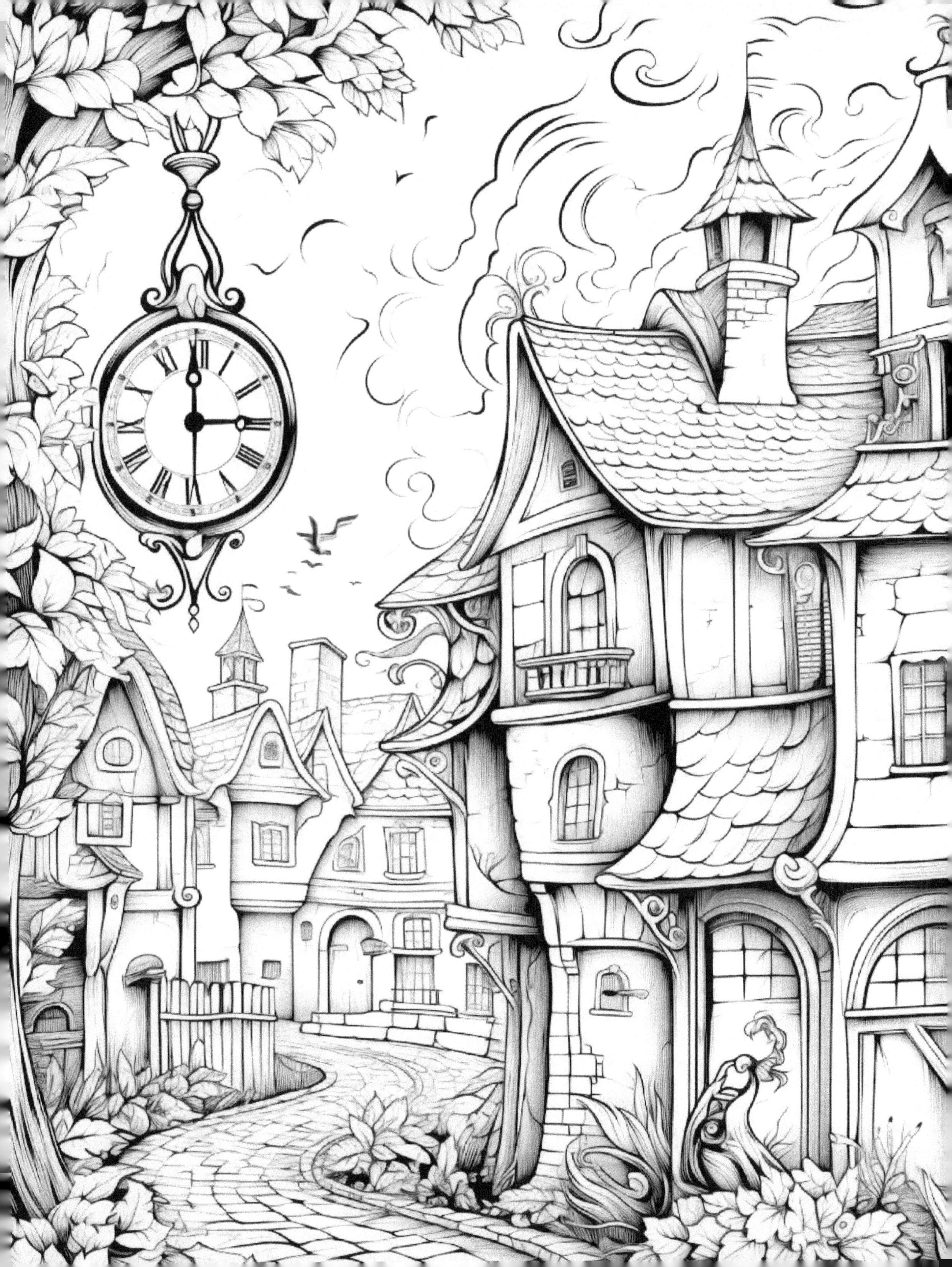

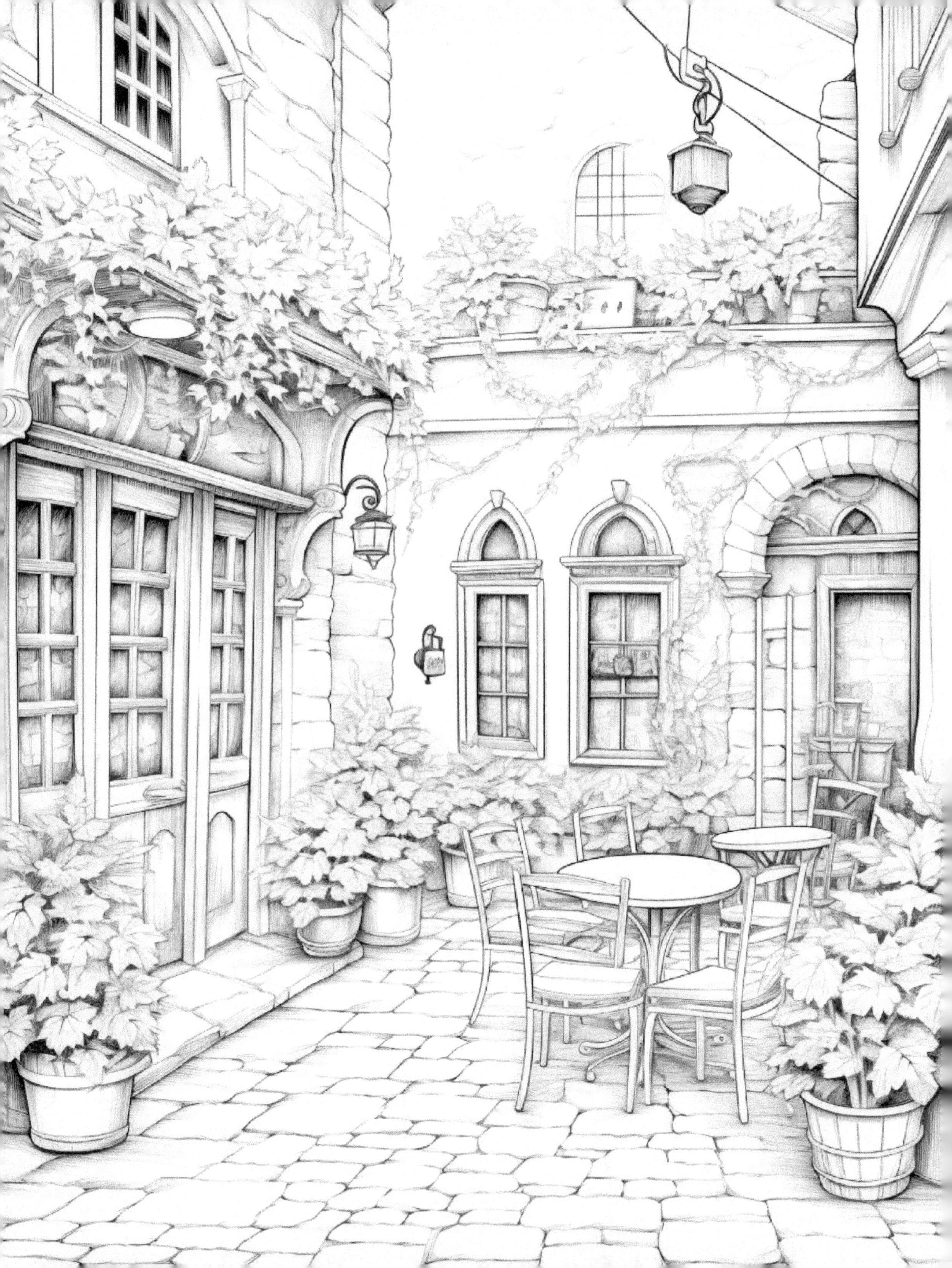

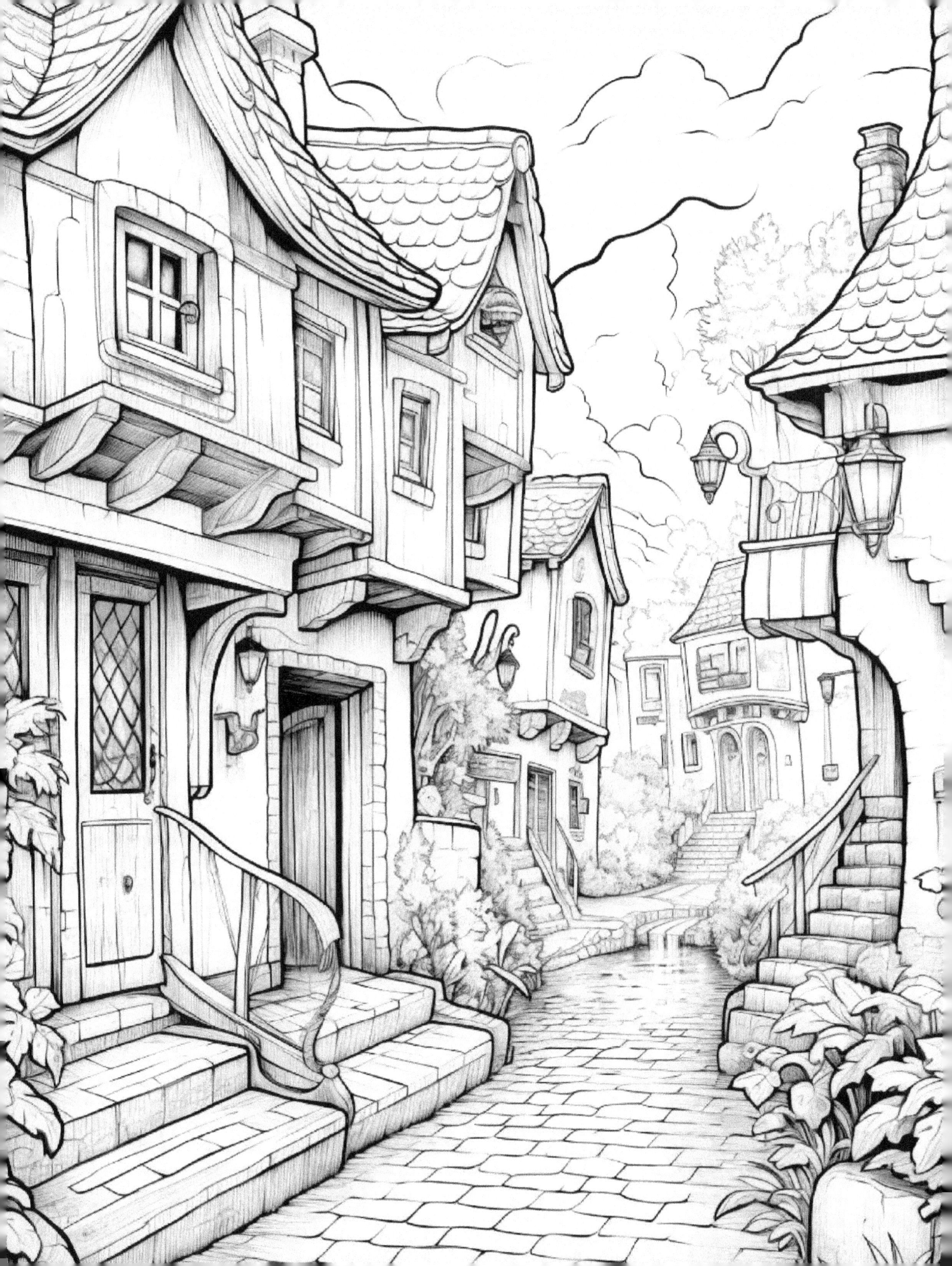

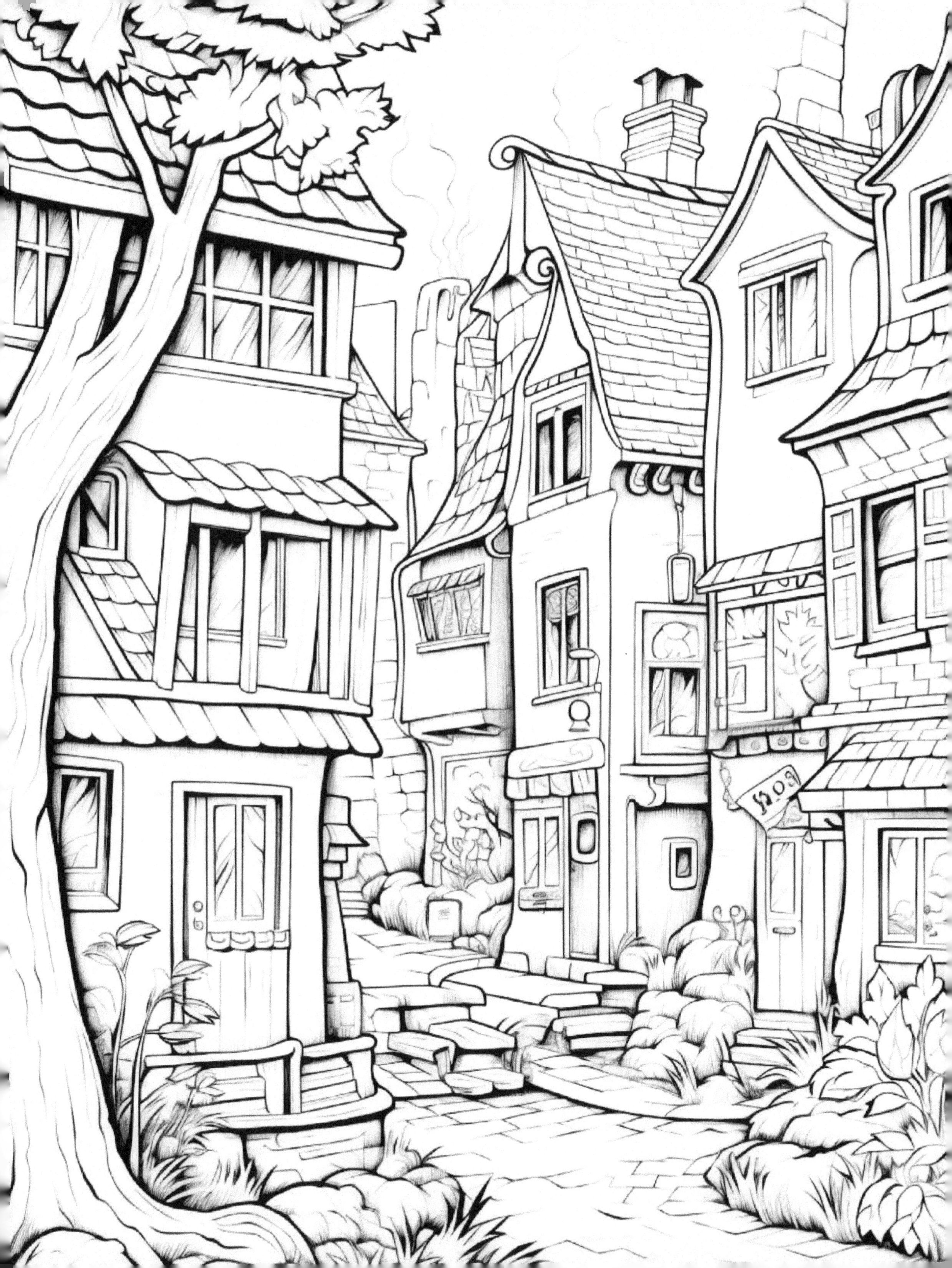

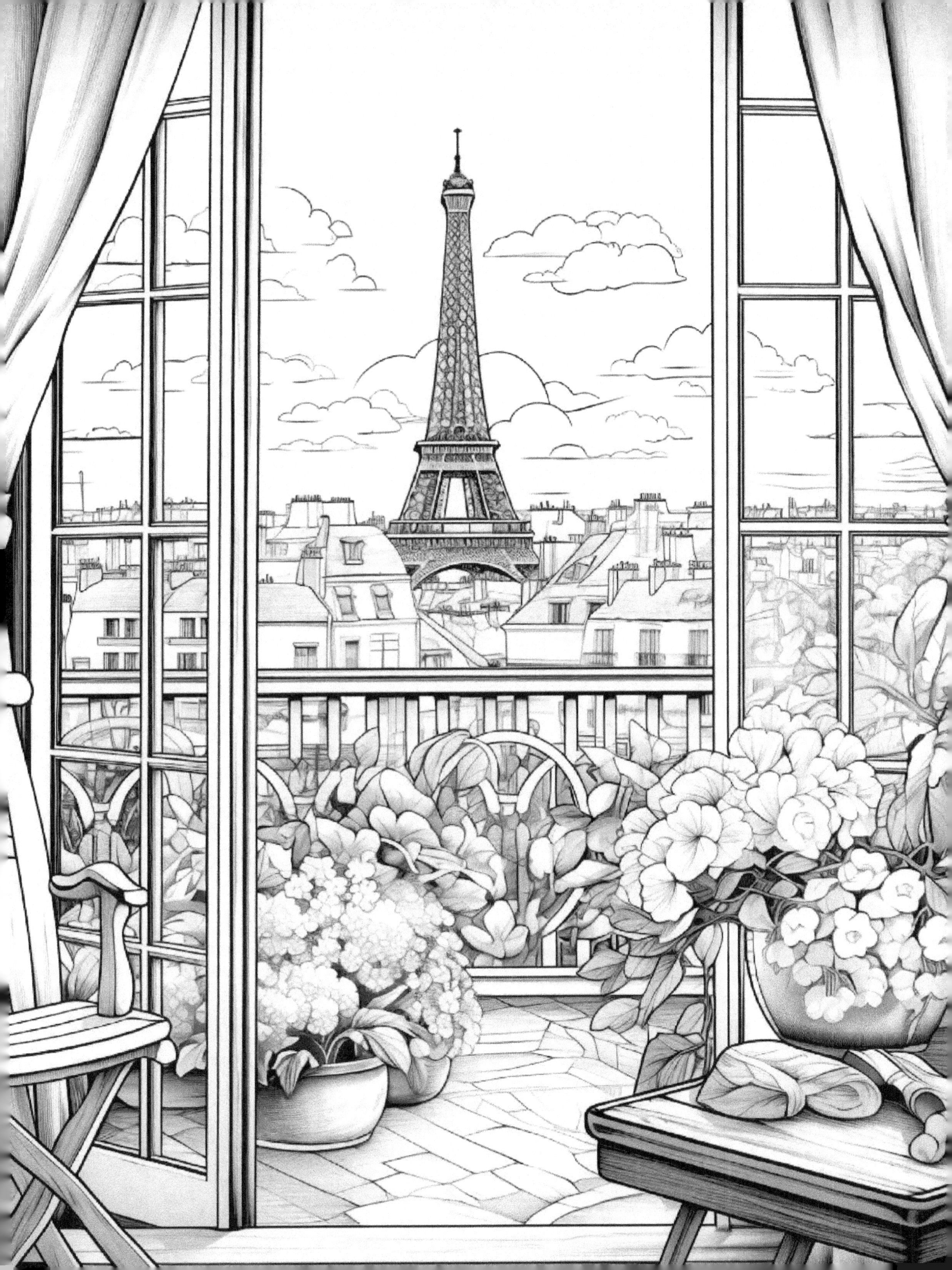

The End